OPEN HOUSE

ALSO BY DREW HAYDEN TAYLOR

PLAYS

*alterNatives**
*The Baby Blues**
*The Berlin Blues**
The Bootlegger Blues
*The Boy in the Treehouse / Girl Who Loved Her Horses**
*The Buz'Gem Blues**
*Cerulean Blue**
*Cottagers and Indians**
*Crees in the Caribbean**
*Dead White Writer on the Floor**
*400 Kilometres**
*God and the Indian**
*In a World Created by a Drunken God**
*Only Drunks and Children Tell the Truth**
*Sir John A: Acts of a Gentrified Ojibway Rebellion**
Someday
Toronto at Dreamer's Rock / Education Is Our Right

FICTION

*Fearless Warriors**
Motorcycles and Sweetgrass
The Night Wanderer
The Night Wanderer: A Graphic Novel (with Alison Kooistra and Michael Wyatt)
Take Us to Your Chief and Other Stories
Chasing Painted Horses
Cold

NON-FICTION

FUNNY, YOU DON'T LOOK LIKE ONE SERIES:
Funny, You Don't Look Like One: Observations of a Blue-Eyed Ojibway
Further Adventures of a Blue-Eyed Ojibway
Furious Observations of a Blue-Eyed Ojibway
Futile Observations of a Blue-Eyed Ojibway
The Best of Funny You Don't Look Like One
Me Artsy
Me Funny
Me Sexy
*NEWS: Postcards from the Four Directions**
Voices: Being Native in Canada (with Linda Jaine)

* Published by Talonbooks

PRAISE FOR DREW HAYDEN TAYLOR'S PREVIOUS PLAYS

Cottagers and Indians

"A deft touch for mixing comedy and commentary in an entertaining, all-Canadian form of social satire."—***The Vancouver Sun***

"Hayden Taylor's play provides a powerful argument that relations between Canada and Indigenous people can become a life-giving force. However, the terms of this relationship must be based on Indigenous sovereignty over land."—***Canadian Literature***

Crees in the Caribbean

"The play is packed with wit and humour, but also packs an emotional punch. At the heart of *Crees in the Caribbean* is a commentary on the universality of human experiences from culture to culture; it shows that people from all parts of the world can share similar stories and experiences."—***The Argus***

In a World Created by a Drunken God

Short-listed for the 2006 Governor General's Literary Award for Drama

"Drew Hayden Taylor adheres to the dictates of classic, riveting theatre by presenting stellar characters struggling with hardcore moral questions, while inviting the audience to continue the dialogue after the curtain has dropped ... Masterful."—***Quill & Quire***

God and the Indian

"A respectful treatment of one of the most painful chapters in Canadian history ... We need to hear the stories Taylor is telling in *God and the Indian*."—***The Georgia Straight***

The Berlin Blues

"Drew Hayden Taylor has produced an accomplished series of comedies about reserve life that are consummate in their dramatic mechanics ... *The Berlin Blues* may be breezy sitcom, but it has a point to make and is masterfully done."—***Canadian Literature***

OPEN HOUSE

A PLAY

DREW HAYDEN TAYLOR

TALONBOOKS

Talonbooks
9259 Shaughnessy Street, Vancouver, British Columbia, Canada V6P 6R4
talonbooks.com

Talonbooks is located on xʷməθkʷəy̓əm, Sḵwx̱wú7mesh, and səlilwətaɬ Lands.

First printing: 2025

Typeset in Minion
Printed and bound in Canada on 100% post-consumer recycled paper

Cover image by Wildpixel via iStock Photo

Talonbooks acknowledges the financial support of the Canada Council for the Arts, the Government of Canada through the Canada Book Fund, and the Province of British Columbia through the British Columbia Arts Council and the Book Publishing Tax Credit.

Library and Archives Canada Cataloguing in Publication

Title: Open house : a play / Drew Hayden Taylor.
Names: Taylor, Drew Hayden, 1962- author
Identifiers: Canadiana 20240459326 | ISBN 9781772016567 (softcover)
Subjects: LCGFT: Drama.
Classification: LCC PS8589.A885 O64 2025 | DDC C812/.54—dc23

To Janine, who makes all things possible

INTRODUCTION

At one point I was going to call this play *Poking the Bear*, for obvious reasons. For the last little while, there's been a lot of media coverage coming out about wokeness and who was allowed to write what about whom, and why. And granted, as a First Nations writer, I was frequently part of this discussion.

The idea for writing a play from several different cultural perspectives had always intrigued me, so an amorphous concept of this play had been bouncing around in my head for a while. It was a project I planned to create sometime down the road. But that road came a lot closer when Derek Ritschel, artistic director of Lighthouse Theatre in Port Dover, Ontario, approached me about writing something along similar lines.

So I put pen to paper … or more accurately fingers to keyboard … and wrote *Open House*. I knew the potential political volatility of somebody writing about somebody else's cultural background, let alone five people's, might be tricky, so I tried to be honest and true to each character's origins. I relied heavily on the actors involved in the various workshops to keep me honest and true. Luckily, being a huge fan and student of history, a lot of the information was already running around in my head.

Essentially this play is a discussion, if not an argument, about which ethnic group has been the most discriminated against in Canadian history. I'm sure you can already see the sparks flying. Choosing the representatives was, in its own way, both difficult and easy. I have one African Canadian, one Chinese Canadian, one Jewish lesbian, one Mohawk lesbian, and a settler (Celtic in case you are curious about specifics). I don't think there is a winner or a loser in these kinds of deliberations. Merely participants.

And obviously, a play of this kind would have to be a comedy … or at least have a lot of comedic elements within its construction to keep the issues palatable.

Regardless, as sometimes happens in the development and production of a play, Infinithéâtre in Montréal became a welcome part of the production discussion, and eventually they were the first to produce it.

So thanks to Lighthouse Theatre for igniting the fire and Infinithéâtre for feeding the flames. I'm very proud of this play. It asks some difficult questions while hopefully making you laugh. I am sending out a Chinese Canadian, African Canadian, Jewish, Mohawk, and Celtic thank you to all the people involved in this production. Special thanks to Zach Fraser, the artistic director of Infinithéâtre, Guy Sprung, the emeritus A.D. of Infinithéâtre, and of course the brilliant Dian Marie Bridge, who directed my mess into a very enjoyable evening of theatre.

Ch'meegwetch to all.

—DREW HAYDEN TAYLOR

Curve Lake First Nation, July 2024

PRODUCTION HISTORY

Open House was first produced from April 18 to 28, 2024, by Infinithéâtre at Factory Studios in Montréal, Québec, with the following cast and crew:

EVE	Rebecca Gibian
TAMMY	Kerrin-Lee Whyte
RUTH	Cara Rebecca
ADRIAN	Christian Paul
NED	Jovanni Sy

Director and Dramaturge	Dian Marie Bridge
Sound Designer	Jesse Ash
Costume Designer	Elisabeth de Medeiros
Set Designer	Joanna Gourdin
Lighting Designer	Tim Rodrigues
Associate Lighting Designer and Technical Director	Aurora Torok
Stage Manager	Danielle Skene
Apprentice Stage Manager	Corey Weiser
Head Tech	Amber Hood
Production Manager	Tristynn Duheme
Production Assistant	Trinity McQuillan

Open House was developed in large part thanks to a commission grant from The Cole Foundation, which allowed Infinithéâtre to invite Drew Hayden Taylor as the inaugural artist-in-residence during their 2021–2022 season.

Several artists contributed to the dramaturgical development of *Open House*, including: Derek Ritschel, Guy Sprung, Diane Roberts, Zach Fraser, Heather White, Adrianne Richards, Tristan D. Lalla, Alex Weiner, Etienne Lou, Jonathan Silver, Stephanie Buxton, Schubert Pierre-Louis, Sophie Gee, Albert Kwan, Nate Blander, and Jonah Blander.

CHARACTERS

EVE Rhodes: Caucasian. Mid-fifties. Real estate agent.

TAMMY Maracle-Brummer: Kanien'kehá:ka (Mohawk). Mid-thirties. Married to Ruth. Pregnant.

RUTH Brummer: Jewish. Late thirties. Married to Tammy. Owns and operates three Starbucks franchises.

ADRIAN Marshal: African Canadian. Late thirties. Chef. Married.

Ning (NED) Leong: Chinese Canadian. Early forties. Lawyer. Recently divorced. He is stylish and full of energy.

LOCATION

A house for sale in a metropolitan suburb.

TIME

There's no time like the present.

LAND ACKNOWLEDGMENT

For the opening of this play in Montréal, I was asked about a Land acknowledgment. There seems to be a bit of a controversy out there about their function and usefulness, so I was asked my opinion on the topic, and if I wanted to write one myself.

I thought, "Why not?"

So I did.

We acknowledge we are on the Traditional Lands of the Kanien'kehá:ka Nation, in a province that maintains French as the official language, in a country that still has strong political and judicial ties to Britain, beside another country whose overpowering pop culture constantly pours across the border. I did once meet a guy who swore up and down the Vikings were here before any Indigenous people ... so, there you go ...

OPEN HOUSE

Lights up revealing the ground floor of a lovely house in an affluent suburb. The living room, which includes a large window, has been immaculately but sparsely staged for potential clients. Also, a tray of leftover cheeses can be seen. Beside it are several half-empty bottles of wine. EVE is pacing back and forth, talking in a very theatrical manner, a manuscript in her hand. At one point, in mid-monologue, she straightens some knick-knacks, notices a flaw on the table, and immediately cleans it.

EVE

I don't love you, Charles. You must know that. I did once. And it was an honest and true love. But now it's gone. Like your hair. It's been said the human body replaces every single cell at least once every seven years. I'm a new woman, Charles. And this new woman ... she isn't interested in the things she was seven years ago. It's time we go our separate ways. We both knew it was only a matter of time. You can keep the dog, I want the kids. Don't say anything, please. Don't cheapen this moment with anger or pleading. Accept it. I'll send Carlos to pick up my things. And Charles ... and I mean this ... I hope your operation goes well ...

She stops for a second, then tries another tack of delivery.

And Charles ... and I mean this ... I hope your operation goes well ...

Not happy, she tries a third time.

... and Charles ... and I mean this ... I hope your operation goes well.

Frustrated with her performance, she tosses the script down. She looks at the empty house.

EVE
(*to herself*) Well, I think that's enough for now.

Gathering up her things, she starts to turn some lights off but notices she is missing something.

EVE
Dammit. My coat.

She checks her watch and runs upstairs. Almost immediately, the door opens and ADRIAN enters, on his phone. He looks around.

ADRIAN
Yeah honey, I'm inside. It looks pretty good so far. Nice flooring. You'd like it. The colour? Okay, picture a chocolate soufflé fresh out of the oven. (*pause*) Don't worry, I know. I won't make any offers till we discuss it. But it has character. I have a good feeling about this. I think you'll love it. Brick exterior, what looks like a renovated front porch. (*pause*) Yeah, yeah I know. I'll do that right now. You'll see what I mean. (*pause*) I did not lose the semi-detached. I just don't like semi-detached. You never know what you'll hear through the walls. (*pause*) Yes, I know you're humouring me on this, but. (*pause*) Okay, talk to you later. Love you.

ADRIAN hangs up, then turns his phone into a camera. He starts taking pictures of various parts of the room. EVE enters with her coat, noticing him.

EVE
Hello. Welcome.

ADRIAN

Please tell me this is the open house?! Otherwise, I've just committed a B and E and ... ooh, is that cheese? I know that's rude, but I haven't eaten all afternoon.

ADRIAN sends the pictures off on his phone.

EVE

Yes to both questions. Help yourself. And welcome. I'm Eve Rhodes, realtor for the family selling the house. Uh, it's quite late. I was going to lock up. If you're still interested, we'll be having another one on Wednesday if you want.

ADRIAN grabs some cheese and crackers. He's not overwhelmed by their quality.

ADRIAN

Thanks, but can I take just a quick peek around? Please? I've been looking at houses all day, and my wife will kill me if I don't give her a report on this place. Housing in this city is insane. But it seems I've saved the best for last. We're from Vancouver. Houses are quite different here.

EVE hesitates.

ADRIAN

Really, it won't take long.

EVE

Why not? My husband says real estate is like basketball, things don't get really exciting until the last ten minutes. And if you have any questions ...

ADRIAN

I'm sure there'll be lots of questions, but probably not from me. My wife tells me I'm just around to open jars and carry luggage. That is her definition of a husband.

EVE
Oh that can't be true. Well, I'm here if you ...

ADRIAN's phone goes off.

ADRIAN
Only twenty seconds. A new record. Always has questions, but I love her for her inquisitive mind. (*answering*) You got them. And. (*pause*) Yes, that is indeed a bay window. I like bay windows. (*pause*) Yes, we can have it renovated if necessary. The walls ... ivory. (*pause*) They look ivory to me. (*pause*) I know what ivory is. (*pause*) Okay, maybe it's off-ivory. That's a colour, isn't it?

EVE is about to answer, but ADRIAN continues, looking through the window.

ADRIAN
Of course we can paint over it. I never doubted that for a second. (*pause*) Uh, sure. Just a second. Uh, Ms. ... Rhodes, was it? What can you tell us about the next-door neighbours? It seems we can see right into their kitchen.

EVE
The Almantes. First-generation Italian family. Lovely people. Keep to themselves. Grow their own tomatoes. Make their own wine too ... but I wouldn't ... not their strongest talent.

ADRIAN
Okay, no wine from the Italians. There's a statement I'd thought I'd never say. And on the other side?

EVE
The Andersons. Retired couple. Quiet. They love to bake. Originally from a town in Nova Scotia called Truro, but their grandkids are out here so they relocated to ...

ADRIAN
They seem to really like flowers. I mean, really like them.

EVE

I guess there's not much else to do when you're retired. Wait till you see their Christmas decorations.

ADRIAN

Wow, for a realtor, you really did your research. (*to his phone*) Did you hear all that? (*pause*) Good. Look, I'll send you more pictures. (*pause*) You have to see the kitchen, Jen. The things I can do in there. (*pause*) Will do. Bye for now. (*pause*) I understand. Talk to you. (*pause*) Okay sweetie, I won't. (*hanging up*) Well, that should do for a while.

EVE

I'm sorry, you are ...?

ADRIAN

Of course, Adrian Marshal. We ... my wife and I ... her name is Jen ... that's who was on the phone ... are looking at houses. Obviously. We've looked at about a dozen so far with little luck, and like I said, it's mean out there. Houses are there, and then they're gone. Like that. This one ... it looks lovely.

EVE

It's the kind of house you can fall in love with immediately. How long have you and your wife been together?

ADRIAN

Four years ... more or less.

EVE

Children?

ADRIAN

Helps to get a house first, if you know what I mean.

EVE

I do. Now, this house is perfect for professionals or family. Or both. Three bedrooms, or two bedrooms and an office. Your choice. Two bathrooms. Eighteen hundred square feet on two floors, plus the partially finished basement. Parking, and close to all the amenities, including a grocery store two streets over. Or depending on your needs, a liquor store one block over. Regardless, it could also be a lovely investment opportunity to rent out. Would you like a tour?

ADRIAN

Indeed.

ADRIAN's phone rings. He answers.

Hey sweetie. Yep, right now. (*pause*) Do you really think. (*pause*) But that's a little. (*pause*) Right.

ADRIAN hangs up and presses a few buttons on his phone.

So sorry. My wife's in Vancouver looking after the sale of our house there. She wants to tour by FaceTime ... There you are. Hey sweetie. This is Eve. My wife, Jen ...

He points the phone at EVE.

EVE

Uh, hello... Jen ... Welcome. I'm Eve Rhodes. So you'd like to see the house ...

A distant electronic voice can be heard as EVE tries to do the best she can with the situation.

Last major renovation was about eleven years ago.

More indecipherable phone noise.

Mostly the roof and windows. There'd been a harsh rain storm. And a new furnace three or four years earlier.

More phone noise.

Upstairs? Sure. Right this way.

EVE shows ADRIAN the way to the stairway. The electronic voice can be heard again.

ADRIAN
Don't you think that's a little. (*pause*) Looks to be about fourteen or maybe more. (*pause*) The stress of all this is really flaring up your OCD. Right.

ADRIAN starts climbing and counting.

One, two, three, four ...

EVE follows, slightly amused. There is silence for a moment, then a knock at the door. It opens, revealing TAMMY and RUTH.

TAMMY
I think that's adorable. Really, I do, Ruth, but I don't think you're up to it.

RUTH
(*waving a brochure*) Come on. It'll be fun. We can take it together.

TAMMY
I don't want to take it together or separately. I've tried twice before, and you have no idea how hard it is.

RUTH
It can't be any harder than Hebrew, and I've already got a working knowledge of that: הכלב החום רץ במעלה גבעת הדשא*

TAMMY
Okay, what does that mean?

* Pronounced "Ha kelev ha khoom ratz beh mah aleh geevat ha dehsheh."

RUTH
(*proudly*) "The small dog is running up the grassy hill." Nothing to it. How hard can Mohawk be?

TAMMY
I'm sorry ... how hard can WHAT be?

TAMMY waits expectantly.

RUTH
(*taking a deep breath*) Guy-young-a-hey.

TAMMY
Once again, it's Kanien'kehá:ka. Learning the proper name might be a good way to start. I've tried to tell you, it's a completely different language in syntax and structure. It's frustrated far smarter people than you. Like me. I love you for wanting to try, but I think we should put our energy into other things. Like this place. I already love it. It just feels ... right.

RUTH
I don't know ... look at those walls. White is so hard to keep clean. I'm going to keep the brochure anyway. You might change your mind.

TAMMY
I might, but that is not white. I would say ... probably cotton. Maybe snow.

RUTH
There's a difference?

TAMMY
Ah, it's a good thing you're pretty. (*looking around*) Tell you what. I'll teach you some social dancing, the moccasin dance, the rabbit dance, maybe. That will be a lot easier to manage. Why the interest in learning our language all of a sudden?

RUTH

Well, with the baby coming, it's made me more conscious of the things we'll have to teach her ... or him.

TAMMY

Can't say I disapprove of that. (*looking around*) Now normally at an open house there should be somebody here ... with lots of shiny teeth and a capitalistic aura.

They hear footsteps and muffled voices coming from upstairs.

RUTH

Mystery solved. Oh, cheese! You can always tell the quality of the place and people by the finger food they leave out. (*tasting a square*) Hmm, fair-quality cheddar. A bit stale. Doubt it's kosher. Just because it may have been made with kosher milk doesn't mean it's kosher. It has ...

TAMMY explores the first floor with an experienced eye.

TAMMY

Yeah, yeah, being Jewish is complicated. Your bubbie taught me that.

RUTH

Don't do that. Stop trying to being so Jewish ... in public.

TAMMY

Oy vey. Again with the attitude. (*looking around*) And you don't keep kosher. So a moot point.

RUTH

Oh, go blockade something.

This is a time-honoured, familiar jousting between the two. They share a moment acknowledging that.

TAMMY
The house has been staged. No sane person could possibly keep a place this size this clean.

RUTH
I disagree. My mother's kitchen table was perpetually cleaner than an operating table. Meanwhile, I've seen your father gut and clean fish on a table, and half an hour later we'd be eating that fish on it.

TAMMY
Oh, trust me. My mother made sure that table was clean. And shame on you for criticizing an action my people have been practising since well before Time Immemorial. Racist. Did you notice the schools? One at each end of the street. Good omen.

RUTH
How can I be racist? I'm Jewish.

TAMMY
I've known a few female misogynists. In today's society, anybody can be anything. Welcome to Canada. That maple tree out front has me worried. Could be a Manitoba maple. They can be a problem. Shallow roots. I don't like how it's leaning. Could be a problem down the road.

RUTH
Well, maybe ...

Suddenly NED enters through the front door.

NED
Hey, hello.

TAMMY and **RUTH**
Uh, hello/hi.

NED
You two the owners? Selling it yourselves, huh? No commission to deal with. Smart. I can appreciate that. I like the place already. Has a nice family feel to it, but I can work with that. Good open concept. Like that, too. A guy could really feel at home here. It will need some new paint, though. Looks too ... antiseptic. (*looking at the wall colour closely*) What is that? Alabaster?

RUTH
Seriously, that's not white to you?

NED
What am I? A colour blind? Might be egg.

TAMMY
I think it's cotton.

NED
Doubt it. Possibly frost. How negotiable is the price? I can pay in cash. You have it listed at ...

TAMMY
Whoa ... this isn't our place. We're here for the open house.

NED
Shit. Sorry. So I guess ... isn't there supposed to be ... a real estate agent of some sort?

RUTH
That is the tradition, but we haven't ...

EVE enters down the staircase with ADRIAN, who is still on his phone.

ADRIAN
Why does it have to be your office? I need one too.

EVE

The other possibility is ... oh ... welcome ... what a surprise. It's getting kind of late ...

TAMMY

Yeah, we would have been here half an hour ago, but a friend had seen an available house in the West End, and we had to navigate a huge traffic thing on our way back. As the saying goes, "People plan. The Creator laughs."

EVE

Is it bad? The accident, I mean.

TAMMY

Coming in, yes, going out, looked normal.

EVE

(*checking her watch*) Oh good. I can still get to the run-through. You have no idea how insane it's been here. Everybody wants to buy a house these days. Help yourself to some wine and cheese. My name is Eve Rhodes, I am handling this house for the owners, and I can answer any questions you may have. The one-pagers are by the door, and please sign the guest book also by the door, which ...

NED

Will keep us up to date on any developments regarding the sale of the house. Yeah, I know. This ain't my first rodeo, sunshine.

Everybody gives NED a puzzled look, till he realizes what he's said.

NED

Sorry, I did not mean that in a derogatory or sexist manner. Just a colloquial expression I picked up somewhere in my youth. Working on it.

NED grabs a piece of cheese and pours himself a wine.

Regardless, thank you. I know I'm late, but this is my only chance to see the house. So far, I'm impressed. Hmm, Cantal. Lovely.

RUTH
I thought it was cheddar.

NED
No. A lot of people do mistake it for cheddar, though. Gotta know what's what. Ms. ... Rhodes, was it? Can I look around?

TAMMY
Excuse me, we were here first.

EVE
I don't think we were introduced.

TAMMY
I'm Tammy Maracle-Brummer and this is my partner, Ruth.

RUTH is about to speak, but ...

ADRIAN
(*looking up from his phone*) With all due respect, technically, I was here first. (*back to his phone*) Eleven by fourteen feet. No sunken tub, but nice shower. Yes, I have a picture, just give me a second. (*sounding a little frustrated*) Sorry, I'll just be a second.

TAMMY
Okay. Uh, Eve, can we see the backyard? It says here there's a backyard.

EVE
Of course. You'll love it. There are two big trees and five hundred square feet of space. Perfect for social events or even some gardening.

TAMMY
Actually, we're more interested in running-around space. I don't look it quite yet, but ...

TAMMY rubs her tummy happily, indicating she's pregnant.

RUTH
Yes, you do. There's an absolutely adorable bump there. Wanna see the sonogram?

TAMMY
No, she doesn't want to see the sonogram. Ruth, my belly is my business.

RUTH
No, technically now it's our business.

EVE
Well, congratulations. In that case, you'll have lots of space back there. In the past there's been an above-ground pool and a full set of swings. A family can have a lot of fun back there.

TAMMY
Great. (*looking at ADRIAN*) This gentleman seems to be busy for the moment. So, may we?

Preoccupied, ADRIAN nods. EVE, TAMMY, and RUTH move towards the back of the house.

EVE
(*exiting, to ADRIAN and NED*) Would you care to join us? You might ...

NED
In a second. I'm not done with this room yet.

NED slowly wanders around the room, taking it in. It should be indicative of how he approaches everything: methodically and meticulously.

EVE

No problem, feel free to notice the wainscotting. Isn't it to die for? (*to TAMMY and RUTH*) I should mention the previous owners had two children themselves. In fact, I think their initials are carved in the elm out back.

TAMMY

Speaking of which, I have a question about that maple out front ...

TAMMY, EVE, and RUTH exit. ADRIAN is still talking on the phone in a whispered argument. NED, slightly amused by the man, looks around, opens doors, runs up the stairs, and exits. ADRIAN is alone.

ADRIAN

(*into his phone*) I don't know. I don't know. Give me a few minutes to find this stuff out, okay? (*pause*) Yes, I know you like this one now. (*pause*) Yes, it's in our price range, though in this market, asking price is so random, it actually doesn't mean anything. (*pause*) I understand that, (*pause*) but I can't do this with the phone attached to my ear. Okay? I need some elbow room. You look after the house there, and I'll take care of the one here. (*pause*) I'll call you when I leave. We can discuss making an offer then.

With a sigh, ADRIAN ends the call. Taking a deep breath amid the gratifying silence, ADRIAN gathers himself up. He notices the manuscript EVE had read from earlier and casually leafs through it.

ADRIAN

"A Drunken God Descends." A play by Samuel Rhodes. (*pause*) Twenty-fourth draft.

NED reappears.

NED

Anything interesting?

ADRIAN
A play of some sort.

NED refreshes his wine and pours ADRIAN a glass.

NED
Ah, artist types. The lady on the phone ... the wife? The mother? Or the mistress?

ADRIAN
(*accepting the glass*) Thanks. Ah ... the first.

NED
If she's so hands-on about all this, why isn't she here?

ADRIAN
Selling our house in Vancouver. This kind of thing is more her thing. I'm not really a details person, as she so frequently points out.

NED
Vancouver. Got too many relatives there. One of the reasons why I live here. You two moving here?

ADRIAN
I'm already here, renting a very small and rather expensive studio for the moment. You?

NED
Just divorced. Or freed. It's just a matter of semantics. Looking for a place to call my own. I was going to go condo, but I don't know. Spent my whole life either in apartments or condos. Wanted to try something a little different. I mean ... who can argue with a lawn? Love that tree out front. Must be amazing in the fall. (*looking around*) Yeah, I can have a lot of fun here.

ADRIAN
Fun? Who buys a house for fun?

NED

Life is full of phases. This is my buy-a-house-and-have-fun phase.

ADRIAN

Hey, I'm sure you're your own guy, but aren't you a little old for that kind of attitude?

NED

Au contraire, I was raised to be old. In the Chinese community, there are always obligations. Family, cultural, social, etc. It's a long story, but those obligations are never-ending and can quickly age you. So now I am in the process of de-obligating myself. (*toasting*) To the art of de-obligating. So, sounds like you might be interested in putting in a bid?

ADRIAN

Possibly but ... we've made offers on four houses. Not even close. The problem is any offer we have to make is on contingency.

NED

Haven't signed off on the Vancouver place yet?

ADRIAN

Almost. Lots of paperwork. Thus why my wife's out west. So our money is tied up until closing. This house buying isn't as easy as I thought.

NED

Few things are. And by the way, you really shouldn't be sharing your negotiating strategy like that. After all, I may be a competitor.

ADRIAN

Oh yeah, good point ... like I said, my wife is much better at this. And, as of five minutes ago, she really does like this place. So far.

NED
And you?

ADRIAN
Oh it looks lovely. I could be happy here. She's a prof at UBC, starting a new position at U of T. Her mind naturally works like this ... measuring and evaluating things. And with the salary boost at her new position, we can now enjoy the dubious task of house shopping.

NED
What do you do?

ADRIAN
I bask in the glory of my wife. Other than that, I'm a chef at a restaurant downtown. The Longhouse.

NED
The Longhouse?! I love your Baffin Island turbot. Had it last week.

ADRIAN
Thank you. The secret is in the preparation of the wild rice stuffing.

NED
You're talking to a Chinese guy about rice?! You got balls. But cool. I'll Yelp you. Your wife ... sure sounds like a handful. I've made a career out of reading people and even over the phone, it's like maybe she doesn't want to move here.

ADRIAN
Her OCD makes radical changes difficult. But she's adapting. She's moving for me, and I do appreciate that. Luckily, the offer the university made is making the transition more manageable.

NED
The Longhouse is a fabulous restaurant, but gotta be more than just that to drag a reluctant wife across the country.

ADRIAN
Well ...

TAMMY and RUTH return to the living room, followed by EVE.

EVE
The fence may need replacing in a few years, but you can worry about that later.

RUTH
I could see Adam running around out there. I think he'd like it.

EVE
I've always loved the name Adam.

TAMMY
Adam?! We haven't discussed names yet.

RUTH
Well ... my mother and I have. You know, just discussing possibilities.

TAMMY
Of course you would have. Ruth, it's a good thing you're smart.

RUTH
Smart enough to find those comments kinda patronizing.

TAMMY
Really? I've heard your bubbie call you both pretty and smart. And from what I've seen, she carries a lot of weight in your family. So you got a problem, take it up with her. Man, I thought Haudenosaunee women could be pushy.

EVE
Haudeno ... I'm sorry.

TAMMY

Haudenosaunee. Or more specifically. Kanien'kehá:ka. Or to the lesser informed, Mohawks.

EVE

Oh, I thought you were Jewish.

TAMMY

Yeah, she's one of the chosen people, I'm Mohawk, a lady of the flint, if you please.

NED

That's an odd mixture.

TAMMY

Robbie Robertson was half-and-half. Kinda what we call a Schmohawk.

TAMMY's expecting a laugh but doesn't get one. Things get awkward.

RUTH

Or Schlomohawks?

Still nothing. Off in the distance, crickets can be heard in the silence.

TAMMY

That kills at the Powwows and Pesach. (*to RUTH*) I don't want our child named after a character in the Bible.

RUTH

Your father is named Isaac. And technically it doesn't come from the Bible. It's from the Torah.

TAMMY

Tomato, tomahto.

RUTH
There are so many who might argue that point. On both sides.

EVE
Well, congratulations on your baby.

NED
Uh, can I take that tour now?

RUTH
We still have to see upstairs.

ADRIAN
Excuse me. I was here first.

ADRIAN's phone rings.

Fuck! (*answering*) I haven't left yet! (*pause, then to EVE*) Uh, my wife wants to know more about this land, where the house is, uh, what it was before it was developed.

TAMMY
It was and is on Indigenous Land. But then again, what isn't?

RUTH rolls her eyes but smiles. EVE gives an awkward smile.

EVE
Hey everyone, look at the crown mouldings.

RUTH
Why do you have to always bring up land issues?

TAMMY
Because it is at the root of so much colonialism. In the end, it all comes down to the Land. And as if Jews don't have their own land issues.

RUTH
That's different.

TAMMY
So you keep saying.

RUTH
Because you don't want to listen.

EVE
Well, this area was developed about ninety years ago, and this particular house was constructed ... maybe ... forty years ago or so.

ADRIAN
Wait a minute. I want to get back to this Indigenous Land thing. This is part of a reserve? There are no reserves or issues like that in this city ... are there? I mean, in Vancouver there were two ...

TAMMY
Reserves, no. But there's more to the Indigenous universe than just reserves. Originally, if you go back far enough, some claim this was probably Anishinaabe Land, maybe even Wendat, or one of the smaller subtribes like the Neutral or Tobacco, but most Haudenosaunee think this was our original hunting grounds. We'd canoe over, bag a deer, and be back home for corn soup by dark.

NED
Oh. Is that a fact?

They all look to EVE.

EVE
Possibly ...?

TAMMY

Let's face it, every house you look at in this country was originally on Indigenous Land.

RUTH sighs.

TAMMY

I heard that.

ADRIAN

(*into his phone*) I think they're talking about Native issues or something. I'm not sure but ... but yes, there is parking ...

TAMMY

Any place there were Indigenous cultures and then colonization, there will always be issues like this. People need to know this shit. Canadians should understand that by now.

NED

My Christ, an optimist! Canadians don't know shit. The longer they're in this country, the more they forget about their past. You know how many times I've had people say, "Why don't you go back to your country?" And I can trace back one set of my great-grandparents longer than most white Canadians.

A flashing light from a police car plays across the curtains. EVE is the only one that notices it. She tries to focus everybody.

EVE

If you'll notice the floor, according to the owners, that is authentic Russian Baltic birch. You don't see that every day.

NED

Russian Baltic birch ... never heard of it. Is that real?

EVE

Oh yes. Very hard to get.

ADRIAN

I'm sorry to interrupt but, just to be absolutely clear, because my wife will want the details, but there are no issues here involving Indigenous ownership of this particular land here. This house? Right? I mean ... we'd just like to avoid any potential future complications.

EVE

No. There are no issues at all.

TAMMY

Well, that's not entirely true. Most major cities in Canada are, from an Aboriginal perspective, on questionably obtained land. If there was a treaty involved, there is usually some discussion about how fair that treaty was.

ADRIAN

Oh fuck, (*listening to the phone*) you are not going to believe this ...

RUTH

Uh, you'll have to excuse Tammy, she ...

TAMMY

"She" what? Ruth, can I see you a moment?

TAMMY pulls RUTH aside.

RUTH

What?

TAMMY

What are you doing?

RUTH

What do you mean "what am I doing"? Not every situation requires a monologue on Indigenous history. Why do you have to keep doing ...

TAMMY

Don't be such a schmuck. I'm doing this to scare them off. Get it?

RUTH clues in.

RUTH

You are amazing.

TAMMY

You know, in Kanien'kéha, both the words "amazing" and "woman" sound amazingly similar.

RUTH

That is so cool! This is why I want to learn ...

TAMMY

(*whispering*) Of course they don't. I made that up. You'll believe anything ... as will they.

TAMMY and RUTH share a fun moment. Suddenly more police lights go whizzing by. ADRIAN notices them this time.

RUTH

(*playing along*) I think I saw some arrowheads in that very backyard.

ADRIAN steps up to the window.

ADRIAN

Uh ... just a second, sweetheart. (*lowering his phone*) Uh, quick question, Ms. Rhodes, those appear to be police cars in front of that house down the street?! Several of them, in fact.

EVE

What? Police cars? I don't think ...

ALL rush to the windows and look out.

RUTH

Those are police cars!

NED

(*to EVE*) They seem to be in front of that split-level duplex at the end of the street ... something we should know about, Ms. Rhodes? A local meth lab or brothel, maybe?

EVE

Of course not. It's a good family community here. I know that house. That's the Sprungs. Their basement has a lovely indoor sauna with marble inlay. I'm sure it's just a misunderstanding.

ADRIAN

Three police cars is not a misunderstanding.

NED

Four.

TAMMY

Five.

EVE

Just calm down, everybody. I assure you this is very unusual for this neighbourhood.

RUTH

How can you be so sure?

EVE

Well, uh ...

ADRIAN

(*to his phone*) Police cars, Jen. Lots of them.

ADRIAN holds up the phone so his wife can see on FaceTime. EVE can feel the shift in concerns and takes charge.

EVE

Everybody just stay here. I'll ... I'll go and see what the difficulty is.

EVE opens the door and exits. The others huddle around the window. EVE immediately returns, grabbing the plate of cheese.

EVE

It's not doughnuts, but ... might help.

Once again EVE exits. The others watch for a few seconds. Another police vehicle rolls by.

ADRIAN

(*to his phone*) I'll call you back. (*to everybody*) That's ... that's a lot of cops.

ADRIAN hangs up.

NED

One of the unexpected advantages of living in a white neighbourhood. Excellent police response time.

TAMMY

(*sarcastically*) Yeah. Thank heavens for small mercies, I guess.

ADRIAN

This can't be good.

NED

What? Did you rob a bank, or wouldn't your wife let you?

ADRIAN

Very funny. There's an awful lot of cops out there. With guns. And tasers. And handcuffs. Other cop-like things.

NED

Yeah, and ...

ADRIAN

I'm Black. And you know police and how they feel about Black people. Like a state sponsored whack-a-mole contest.

NED

I'm Chinese, so what? You're well-dressed. Well groomed. And appear well-educated. From BC. What are you, "Straight Outta" Richmond?

ADRIAN

No. Burnaby. I get the reference, but not every Black person is fond of hip hop. And yes, I did have a suburban childhood. The unfortunate thing is ... do you know how many Black people live in Vancouver proper? Not a lot. That's one of the reasons I wanted to move out here. It's good to see some darker faces on the streets and in the stores. But I don't think the police feel that way.

NED

Ah, you've got nothing to be afraid of.

ADRIAN

You've never been Black, have you?

NED

What do you think?

ADRIAN

People watch you in stores. People think you have access to all kinds of drugs. Or are great at basketball or football. My father worked for Bell Canada for twenty-three years. My mother, a housewife who occasionally did some work for her church. As for the sports, I have asthma. I know the secret to a perfectly made omelette, which is harder than you think, but last week I was pulled over by the cops. For no reason. Second time in as many months. A DWB, "driving while Black." Guilty by abundant melanin.

TAMMY

I hear you. Indigenous people are 5 percent of the population, but we're 30 percent or more of the prison population. It's like white people are afraid of the dark, both literally and figuratively.

ADRIAN

And yet they will spend tens of thousands of dollars to spray tan, sit in a tanning machine, or travel the world in search of a darker tan.

TAMMY

(*shaking her head*) Yeah, white people. They can be a conundrum.

NED

(*to RUTH*) And you? She said you were Jewish. You afraid of the men in blue?

RUTH

(*shrugging*) On a larger, national scale, sometimes. But when a sizable chunk of the population believes you're part of an international cabal secretly running the finances of the world, and somebody robs a local convenience store, they don't usually think of Jews. They believe we subcontract that kind of thing. Men in blue, no. Men in brown shirts, yes. (*to NED*) You don't seem worried.

NED

Me? Nah. Unless they've watched too many karate movies and think all Chinese are secretly part of some Triad. Or the cops are hungry for some chow mein.

ADRIAN

Isn't karate Japanese?

RUTH

Yeah, it's kung fu. That's Chinese, isn't it?

NED

I can't believe I'm having this conversation.

ADRIAN

Do Jews have a martial art?

RUTH

Yep, it's called wandering the desert for forty years. I've always thought that was more effective than Krav Maga.

NED

(*checking his watch*) Man, I hope we can speed this up.

RUTH

Oh, now you're in a hurry?

NED

As a matter of fact, I am. My son plays on a hockey team. His game starts in an hour.

TAMMY

Nice to see a man share time with his son. Don't really see that a lot anymore.

NED

Since the divorce, I try to be as much a part of his life as I can. He ... he needs me. That's one of the reasons I want to buy this place. A good family man should have a good family home.

ADRIAN

So you are going to put an offer down on this house?

NED

Should I clear it with your wife first? Just kidding. It's exactly what I'm looking for. I can see it happening. (*looking out the window and seeing more cars going by*) Must be something really interesting happening over there. What bad things do white people do? My money's on a Ponzi scheme or something like that.

ADRIAN

Yeah, that sounds very Caucasian. Or maybe rigging polo games.

TAMMY

I've heard that! I've heard that.

RUTH

Serial killers?

TAMMY

Yeah, yeah! Statistically most of them are white. They're very good at that.

ADRIAN

And yet the police prefer to pull me over!

RUTH

(*whispering to TAMMY*) Tammy, if you're willing to pull the Indigenous Land card, I'm getting the impression you more than like this place. You want this place.

TAMMY

Yes I do. Definitely. It has everything ...

RUTH

But?

TAMMY

It's just a little weird for me. I mean it's the first house I ... or we have ever bought. As an Indigenous woman. I mean ... there's something uncomfortably ironic about purchasing a chunk of land that used to be ours to begin with. Kind of like buying back a car that was stolen from you. I can almost hear my Ancestors telling me, "Don't do it! It's a trap! Don't accept any blankets." But I think the bids are not technically due till Wednesday.

RUTH

Buying and selling things ... now that's my cultural bailiwick. Don't panic, we have our pre-approved mortgage. We can handle it.

TAMMY

We should have asked for more.

RUTH

They wouldn't give us more. I'm the only one working, remember? It'll be enough.

TAMMY

I heard what your brother said. Getting a pre-approved mortgage may be essential, but it's like graduating high school these days. It's not the be-all and end-all it once was. It might not be enough.

RUTH

If worst comes to worst, maybe our parents can top it up. I don't know about Mohawks, but when it comes to Jews, having grandkids is like having an ATM card.

TAMMY

Yeah, my grandparents have more love than money to offer, but culturally, we're rich. I guess ethnically, it will be corn soup versus chicken soup.

RUTH

Yeah, a Jewish grandmother versus a Mohawk grandmother. Kinda like Superman versus the Incredible Hulk.

NED

(*refilling his wine and overhearing*) Don't mean to pee in your Rice Krispies, guys, but you shouldn't take a dump without a pre-authorized anything. Never, ever spend your own money.

TAMMY

Excuse me, but this is a private matter.

NED

Then go someplace private. This is the fifth house I've looked at and by far the best. Just giving you a heads-up. I'm going for it. I've already done the due diligence.

RUTH

You're awfully confident of yourself.

NED

Well, when you're raised by an immigrant family in a new country, you can either be fearful or confident. I thought confidence was the better of the two options.

ADRIAN, sitting on the stairs, is busy texting. NED notices.

NED

Say hello for me.

ADRIAN

Where the fuck is your attitude coming from, dude? Buying a house is a joint decision. Keeping her informed of everything shouldn't be a problem. What is it to you?

NED

Absolutely nothing.

RUTH

I'm gonna say ... freshly divorced?

NED

I guess it shows. The paint's still wet. I'm thirty-eight and for the first time in my life, I am on my own and making my own decisions. And I like it. L'chaim.

ADRIAN

Just can the attitude, will you? We all have our strengths. This kinda thing is my wife's. I'm the more artistic of the two, and to tell you the truth, these kinds of decisions bore the hell out of me. I have no trouble relying on Jen for her input in situations like this. In fact, I welcome it. Complain all you want, dude, but at least at the end of the day, I have somebody to go home to and discuss these things with ... if she were actually in this city at the moment.

NED smiles and drinks.

TAMMY
What if we want to put in a bid?

NED
You go right ahead. Free country and all that.

RUTH
Something tells me you doubt we'd have a chance.

NED smiles.

NED
Like I said, it's a free country.

TAMMY
Is it? Is it really? How naive.

NED
Okay then, it's a freer country than some others. How's that? (*looking out the window*) I've got to go soon.

TAMMY
You're free to leave.

NED
Very funny. Look, I know you Indigenous people have issues with Canada. That's fine and cool ...

TAMMY
Fine and cool?! Thanks!

NED

But compared with how my grandparents and great-grandparents lived and what they had to do, I think things are pretty good today, by comparison. I'd rather be living here, now, then back when they got here. A hundred years ago I probably wouldn't be allowed in this neighbourhood, unless somebody wanted their laundry done.

ADRIAN

He's not wrong. There are a thousand things wrong with this country, this society, but like he said, a hundred years ago, you think my wife and I would be allowed to even set foot in a house like this?

RUTH

(*raising her hand*) Hello. Jew! We've all got issues with Canadian history.

NED

I know the argument. We're all bricks in the flawed building that is Canada. The scars are plentiful and deep. I'm sure everybody here is familiar with the famous Chinese head tax, where we had to pay an exorbitant fee for the privilege of immigrating here. That in itself was reprehensible, but ever heard of the Chinese Exclusion Act? It was officially known as the Chinese Immigration Act. Essentially, Chinese immigration was banned, with only fifteen privileged individuals admitted during the act's twenty-four-year span. Do you like irony? Here's the ironic part. It came into effect on July 1st, 1923. July 1st! For a lot of my people, Canada Day is known as "Humiliation Day." In some cities, they lower flags to half-mast and hang mourning wreaths on doors and in shop windows. Today ... and today is what matters, this son of Chinese immigrants has a business that employs twenty-six people. Twenty of them white. And it feels good. So yeah, history sucks, but I'm doing what I can to make today a lot better. And this house, this chunk of Canadian land ... I want to call it my own. And while I have difficulties with many of my family ... and their customs, this way I know their journey will be complete. Little victories are better than no victories.

RUTH

Wow, I think that defines the Canadian experience. For non-WASPs.

NED

It's so fucking weird. Asians are frequently considered model minorities, but we still have to deal with shit. When COVID and SARS hit, we got the dirty looks. It's enough to make you drink ... I mean think.

NED takes a sip. ADRIAN's phone goes off.

ADRIAN

Fuck. (*answering*) Hey sweetie. (*pause*) Yes, honey ... I haven't had a chance. (*pause*) The basement? Ah yeah, I suppose it could be an apartment. I think there's some plumbing that would need to be done. But why, (*pause*) your mother?! Wait a minute, we discussed that. We discussed that a lot, remember. I ...

Embarrassed, ADRIAN dodges into another room. Smirking, NED watches as ADRIAN exits. TAMMY notices. NED then goes to take another drink, but his cup is empty.

TAMMY

You got a problem with a man communicating with his wife?

NED

Just unfortunate flashbacks. I am sure they have a fabulous relationship. Law of averages says one or two must exist out there. Did I hear you say you were Native?

TAMMY

No. You heard me say I was Kanien'kehá:ka. Why?

NED

You know this street used to be called Indian Avenue until they changed the name about eleven ... twelve years ago. Political correctness and all.

RUTH

Son of a ...

TAMMY

What? How do you know that?

NED

Like I said, I did my due diligence on this place. Including its history. I don't just buy houses on a whim. And I don't think they were talking basmati Indian.

RUTH

Oh for ... why are you doing this?

NED

Would moving into a home with that history be a kind of bad karma? (*smiling to himself*) See what I did there ... I juxtaposed the concept of "Indian" ...

Suddenly, EVE enters the house, talking on her phone.

EVE

That's what's happening. I'll get there when I get there. Have somebody read my lines and keep your fingers crossed. (*pause*) Fabulous. Bye for now.

EVE puts her phone away and faces everyone.

EVE

Okay everyone, I'm told no need to worry...

ADRIAN enters, hearing EVE, and puts his phone on mute.

NED
Finally. So, what's happening out there? Can we leave?

EVE
Short answer, no. Seems there's been an "incident." That's all they'll tell me. They're locking the whole street down for the next little while until they get whatever the incident is dealt with. (*pause*) And they ate all my cheese.

NED checks his watch.

NED
Damn it. That's not good enough. I have to go. Eve Rhodes, can I talk to you for a second?

EVE and NED go off to the side.

NED
Look, I don't have time to deal with all this. I know for a fact that Adrian the chef wants to make an offer. Probably the two women, too. Let them. I don't even have to know how much, but I'll top it by ... 8 percent. I just want to make sure you understand that. I'm in for whatever it takes. All right, I'm out of here.

EVE
Uh, no you're not.

NED
Beg your pardon?

EVE
Nobody is going anywhere. As I was told, an "incident" of some sort has occurred. The street is in lockdown. Nobody is being allowed out of their homes.

RUTH
Fuck. We're gonna be late. The Metropolitan Multicultural Services Association doesn't operate on Indian or Jewish time.

Several quizzical looks.

TAMMY

It's an organization that promotes diversity in the city. I volunteer for them. It's awards night, and we have to be there.

EVE

I sympathize, but there's nothing I can do. I was supposed to leave twenty minutes ago myself. The tech run is tonight ...

TAMMY

What's a tech run?

ADRIAN

I think the more important question is what the hell is an "incident"? A six-police-car incident? That seems to me to be more than just an "incident." (*returning to his phone*) Okay Jen, I'm back ...

TAMMY

Excuse me, Ms. Rhodes ... is it true this street used to be called Indian Avenue? I mean, if so, that should have been mentioned in the listing? I mean, I don't think Ruth would be comfortable living on Jew Avenue?

ADRIAN

(*to his phone*) For fuck's sake, Jen, no.

EVE

I'm sorry, but I've lived here ... in this part of the city ... for most of my life. To the best of my knowledge, this street was never renamed. It's always been called ...

TAMMY spots NED smiling.

TAMMY

You made that up!

NED shrugs.

NED

Wow, you would raise a fuss over something that doesn't exist anymore.

ADRIAN's conversation takes place at one side of the apartment while the rest carry on, trying to ignore his rising voice.

ADRIAN

(*to his phone*) I don't want your mother living in our basement. I don't want anybody living in our basement. I was planning on a pool table ...

EVE

Seriously, would that have been a problem? I mean, it's just a name. A name that hasn't been changed.

ADRIAN

(*to his phone*) The novelty of living with people I don't want to evaporated a long time ago.

TAMMY

You probably won't understand, but names and history are important. I know some people who have two or three separate names, some legal, some cultural. They are all important, and they say something. Why wouldn't names on the Land have equal importance?

ADRIAN

(*to his phone*) You're messing with the plan. We ... I repeat we ... me and you, are moving here to start a new life. We've been married four years, Jen. We need to get out of Vancouver. It's too small. It's suffocating. Everybody there wants just seafood and Asian food. And vegan food. And ... and ... you know my journey. Plus, I don't want to live with anybody! (*pause*) Except you, of course.

NED

And why wouldn't I understand that? China and its people are very attached to their country. I don't live in China, but I speak Cantonese. You live here, but do you speak your Mohawk language?

TAMMY

It's a very difficult language. And there's a big difference between being attached to the Land and their country. Don't confuse respect for Mother Earth with nationalism.

EVE

This is getting so complicated. All we're trying to do is sell a house.

RUTH

If I remember correctly, you guys invaded Tibet? And you keep eyeing Taiwan ... I mean I've seen protests ...

NED

Gaza.

There is a silence. EVE crosses over and wearily tries to pour herself some wine. The bottle's empty. She pulls a box of wine out of the closet and opens it.

NED

Wow, that made things go limp.

EVE

I used to live on Hymen Street. I wonder what that implies.

RUTH

Now that's ... that's complicated.

NED

Is that a Mother Earth or a nationalism issue?

ADRIAN

(*to his phone*) Yes Jen, I like the porch. I like the ivory walls. Love Finnish birch flooring. Don't change the ...

EVE

Russian birch! Russian birch!

TAMMY

(*looking at ADRIAN*) I don't think that's the issue.

ADRIAN

(*to his phone*) Fuck this. I'm not a child, Jen. I don't need you constantly looking over my shoulder. I run the best kitchen in the city, and that's enough pressure for any man. As it stands, I get just five hours of sleep a night. Throw your mother into the mix, and I'll be lucky to get three. The mayor and council are coming to the restaurant tomorrow night, and I should be planning that meal instead of chasing houses all across this city. Just ... go live with your mother. (*pause*) This is calm. (*pause*) I will be just fine. (*pause*) Oh yeah! Oh yeah?!

ADRIAN hangs up.

(*to EVE*) I want this house! I want it now. Tell me where to sign.

EVE

It's a little more complicated than that.

NED

Mr. Marshal, real estate, as in business, is frequently not what you have but what people think you have. Play your cards quietly and carefully. Stick to your turbot. Your negotiation skills could use some work. Now, I say fuck the police. I've seen what I wanted to see. I know what I'm going to do. I'm not waiting around for some cop circle jerk. You have my offer.

TAMMY

He made an offer?

ADRIAN
I'll top it by $10,000.

NED
No, you won't.

NED opens the door to leave. EVE peaks around his shoulder.

EVE
Ah sir, the police seem quite serious. You might want to reconsider.

RUTH
Yeah, I wouldn't, if I were you.

NED
Don't be too sure about that. If you were me, you just might.

NED walks out the door. They all watch. Soon a flood of lights comes pouring in through the door, almost blinding, and a loud commanding voice on loudspeaker is heard.

VOICE-OVER
SIR! SIR! PLEASE REMAIN IN YOUR HOUSE. DO NOT ATTEMPT TO LEAVE UNTIL THE ALL CLEAR IS GIVEN. THAT IS A POLICE ORDER. GO BACK INSIDE.

There is a beat, then NED re-enters the house looking a little defeated.

NED
I got as far as the lilac bush. Any more wine?

ADRIAN
Wow, they are really serious.

RUTH
(*to TAMMY*) But we have to leave. We're up first.

NED
Yeah, those multicultural awards won't give themselves away.

RUTH
Maybe we could just hop the fence out back.

TAMMY
Remember me? I'm Tammy Maracle-Brummer, and Mohawk women do not run from cops. Besides, I'm four months pregnant. So there is no fence climbing in my immediate future.

RUTH
Jeez, my great-grandmother dodged bullets and crawled through ditches to get here, all the while carrying my grandfather.

TAMMY
Look, don't you dare play "my history is worse than your history" with me again. You know I can match you story for story.

RUTH
Can you, Tammy? Can you really?

TAMMY
Excuse me?

RUTH
I always have. Sweetheart, I really respect your confidence and inner strength, that is why I married you and a very important reason why we are having a child ... but we're trying to buy a house here. This might not be the right time and place.

NED
Guys, do you have to do that here? I divorced this.

TAMMY
Shut up.

NED

I also divorced that.

ADRIAN

Uh, Ms. Rhodes, if I may change the topic, I have an awkward question.

EVE waits expectantly.

ADRIAN

This neighbourhood. The neighbours ... I'm hoping they won't mind a couple like us moving in here, will they? I mean, I doubt it. But my wife ... she ... she has concerns.

EVE

Oh no, not at all. Black people are more than welcome. It's quite a liberal street. There's a Montessori school just down the street. And a Green Party nominee came in second in the last election. If I may, you're not looking well, Mr. Marshal.

ADRIAN

Yeah, just a little stressed out. We've had some negative experiences in the past. People reacting to us. You spend your whole lives at the bottom of the social ladder, crawling your way up, and no matter what you do or how high you climb, there are still people looking down at you.

EVE

Just because you're Black?

ADRIAN

Well, it's a little more complex than that. My parents used to tell me to get a thicker skin, which I found kinda funny, coming from them. Interesting how frequently things come down to just skin.

EVE

Well, that won't be an issue here. One block over, there's a gay couple.

RUTH
How comforting.

EVE
I mean ...

NED
Interesting how you knew that's what he was talking about.

EVE
What? I don't understand.

NED
What he originally said was ... "won't mind a couple like us moving in here." The way he phrased it, sounds kind of vague. They could have been anything, Unitarians, Wiccans, vegans. But not to you. Like it's been discussed before.

EVE
What are you ... what?

NED
Could be just me, though. (*indicating ADRIAN*) Just like him, I can get paranoid about these things. Chinese people are good for some stir-fried rice and setting up your printer, but living next door or dating your daughter, the smiles get kind of shallow. Sometimes the narrower your eyes, the narrower your chances in this country.

EVE
Not here. Not on this street. Or in this neighbourhood.

ADRIAN
You sound awfully confident.

EVE
I am.

NED
For the sake of argument, do you have friends who are Black?

EVE
As a matter of fact, I do. Several. Chinese people, too.

RUTH
Jews?

EVE
Of course. The Pfeffersteins. Wonderful couple. Make the best rugelach on the block.

RUTH
Are they the only Jews on the block?

EVE
I believe they are.

TAMMY
Any Indigenous people in your rainbow of suburbia?

EVE pauses to think. Her expression falters.

EVE
Uh ... I don't think so. At least none that ... look ... Indigenous. If you know what I mean.

TAMMY
I know what you mean.

NED takes out his phone.

NED
Well people, as interesting as this all is, I do have a life beyond the trials and tribulations of being ethnic in Canada. I have to text my son. Tell him I'll be late for his game. He'll understand. He's a good kid. We'll go for ice cream after. He'll like that.

NED casually walks by EVE and whispers in her ear.

(*winking at EVE*) Remember my offer.

ADRIAN
Hockey ... I wanted to play hockey once, but my parents told me it was too expensive.

NED
Yes. Yes, it can be. Insanely so. Remember that when and if you negotiate your mortgage. I think that's why there are so many white kids in the leagues. Soccer is so much cheaper and, in my opinion, more interesting, but hey, the kid wants to play hockey, so he plays hockey. Nothing more Canadian than Canada's national sport.

TAMMY
Technically lacrosse is Canada's official national sport.

EVE
Really?

TAMMY
Oh yes, and there's a theory hockey was invented by the Mi'kmaq. Supposedly there's documentation. How's that for your Canadian games?

NED
Is that the only channel your conscious mind is tuned to?

TAMMY
The truth? Yes.

NED
I don't know. Truth can be pretty subjective. In fact, subjectivity can be subjective.

RUTH
What the hell does that mean?

NED
I don't know. I was trying for something.

ADRIAN
Your son. What team does he play on? Something that defines the Canadian experience?

NED
They're called the Chiefs.

TAMMY
What?

RUTH
And here we go.

TAMMY
Did you say ... the Chiefs? As in ... Indian Chiefs?

NED
Now you're jumping to conclusions. Could be ... oh ... police chiefs or fire chiefs. There are other chiefs in this universe, you know. Could be the chefs with just a misprinted "I," am I right, Adrian?

TAMMY
Oh really! I don't suppose there's a big-assed Indian head with lots of feathers poking out of it like an afro as their logo?! Huh? Is there? Well? Do a lot of police or fire chiefs wear feathered headdresses?

NED
There's been talk of changing the name. I don't really care, but ...

TAMMY
Of course you don't. Names like that are offensive to people like me.

ADRIAN
Didn't the Edmonton Eskimos change their name?

TAMMY
Do you know what the word "Eskimo" means?! It's a derogatory term meaning "eater of raw meat."

NED
What's wrong with that? Oh man, I could go for some sushi. (*to ADRIAN*) Hey man, I seem to remember some very tasty beef tartare at your restaurant? I'm a proud eater of raw meat.

TAMMY
We are not inanimate objects to be used and bandied about by sports teams. It's dehumanizing. And that dehumanizing effect can spread to all things Indigenous, including us. They don't do it with Jews, with Blacks, with Asians.

NED
The Vikings and the Texans don't mind.

ADRIAN
Don't forget the Fighting Irish. And the Celtics.

RUTH
Ugh, sports people. And Tammy, in all fairness, your brother wears a Cleveland Indians baseball cap.

TAMMY
He wears it ironically. That's completely different. He's making a statement. Like Black people wearing something with the N-word on it.

RUTH
I'm no expert but I don't think the N-word lends itself to irony very easily.

ADRIAN
No. It does not.

TAMMY

This is just one reason why Indigenous people have to be the most oppressed people in this country.

Silence. There is a subtle reaction in the room.

RUTH

(*to herself*) Unlike Jews, who have historically been kicked out of practically every country in the world, but hey, who's counting.

ADRIAN

(*to TAMMY*) I'm sorry?! What did you say?

NED

That's ... That's a hefty claim there, lady. I didn't realize you could measure things like that. And take ownership.

TAMMY

My master's thesis. I spent two years researching and writing it. The evidence is all there, if you know how and where to look.

NED

Again, there's your very specific channel of subjectivity.

ADRIAN

You do realize there is a Black man standing in this house? In this country, quite a few of us might disagree with you. You can stand there claiming some unique relationship to this ... land ... I kinda understand that, but not everybody came to this country willingly.

TAMMY

I know the history. American slaves, the Underground Railroad, etc.

ADRIAN

(*sarcastically*) Good for you. Just because some American slaves ran to Canada for freedom doesn't exclude the fact there used to be slavery here, too. The fact is many of us had little choice in being here, that gives us a unique relationship with this country, too. Ever heard of Maafa? I didn't, but my wife told me about it. It's an African word, sometimes called the African Holocaust. The term goes back to the late '80s. It refers to any atrocity such as slavery, imperialism, colonialism, and other forms of oppression, against Black people, especially when committed by non-Africans. A lot of Black people were forced to come here.

NED
Touché, my man, yet most of the Black people I know weren't descended from escaped American slaves. Most of them speak in a variety of accents from all over the world and would usually prefer a roti rather than chitlins.

ADRIAN
Good point. They are proud to be Canadians. They picked this country. Canada provided them with ...

EVE
Wait, a few minutes ago you were talking about how racist this country is. Now it seems like you're defending it?

ADRIAN pauses, trying to collect his thoughts.

ADRIAN
I did. And I was. Wait, give me a second ...

NED
Need I remind people the Chinese community have had quite a few bumpy roads on our way to being accepted in this country? Some a little more severe than appearing on a hockey jersey.

TAMMY
I didn't say we're the only ones to face oppression and racism. Shit, Canada and colonization have dumped a truckload of horrors on practically all of our people.

ADRIAN
How benevolent of you.

TAMMY
But in the Canadian context, our entire history has been one of racism, oppression, and colonization since contact. Ruth and I have had long conversations about this.

RUTH
Way into the night. But I've always been uncomfortable with your methodology. When you're inside looking out, you only see a small percentage of the picture.

EVE
I can relate. The last election ... my husband and I ... oh the fights we had. It's a good thing they only happen every four or five years. Me Too movement? Hey, I'm a woman. That Black Lives Matter, totally support it. Rage against the machine, I always say!!!!

ADRIAN
Yeah, yeah, good for you. And on behalf of all the Black people in Canada, we thank you. (*to TAMMY and RUTH*) I gotta ask. You two seem so different. How did the two of you hook up, anyways?

NED
Yeah, are there some Jewish-Mohawk lesbian bars I don't know about?

RUTH
She was a student working on her master's. I own a Starbucks franchise. It's a relationship made in heaven. Actually, I operate three Starbucks. That small little bean discovered by Arabs will be financing our house, when we find it.

TAMMY
I think we have.

EVE

So your whole relationship is built on caffeine addiction?!

RUTH

Well, both her culture and my culture are matrilineal. That helped. I come from a long line of bossy women.

TAMMY

And I'm used to being bossy.

NED

Yeah, I've surfed that beach. The novelty wears off. So, what is the Jewish perspective on Mohawks ...

TAMMY

Kanien'kehá:ka.

NED

I stand corrected. As a Jewish woman ... I assume a fairly observant one ...

RUTH

As observant as most Catholics ... for the moment.

NED

Point taken ... how do you feel about your partner there usurping the concept of oppression? Sounds like, as my father used to say, a kick in the pants. Except he said it in Cantonese. Somehow it sounds wiser.

RUTH

I mean, Jews have been oppressed everywhere ... with the possible exception of Antarctica, but then again, who knows? I suppose polar scientists are not immune. Indigenous people don't know what it's like to be hated in foreign lands. Practically all foreign lands. For a substantial period of time. Like, forever. So it's one thing to be hated everywhere, which Indigenous people are not really familiar with. It's another thing to be hated in your own land. So her's is more of a domestic perspective, not an international one. I ... we ... have a broader experience with that kind of oppression. And ... and ... don't get me started on the Holocaust.

EVE

I didn't know we had.

RUTH

Of course, there are those who don't even know there is a problem. A lot of Canadians' only connection with Jews is *The Merchant of Venice* and bagels. But do you want to know the really ironic part of this argument? Indigenous people are loved, adored, embraced in, of all places, Germany. And if you can believe this, back in the 1930s, Hitler delivered a proclamation making North American Aboriginal people honorary Aryans. How's that for your kick in your proverbial pants?

TAMMY

So at least we have that going for us. But that's your uncle talking. He just doesn't like me.

RUTH

He's kind of old school. I don't think he ever got over us getting married. Very old school. Us having a child is gonna throw him for a loop.

TAMMY

It's more than that. He's so hung up on the whole Palestine situation. Especially lately, with the war. It's practically consuming him.

RUTH

Well, he's ... he's ... Jewish.

TAMMY

No, he's Israeli. From what you told me, that can be a big difference. He really needs to get over that whole Palestine situation. This is Canada, we have our own issues of colonization to deal with here.

RUTH
Events in the Middle East cast a pretty big shadow. Tammy, honey ...

ADRIAN
There's an Indigenous perspective on all that's happening over there? That's ... unexpected.

TAMMY
Not really. Think of it this way ... a sizable chunk of Indigenous Canada can relate to being forcibly placed on a small chunk of land on a continent your people have lived on since Time Immemorial. Now their movements are strictly controlled by a larger, better armed, economically more powerful people. Openly controlled and criticized by the state in power. For many First Nations, the similarities are a little too close for comfort. I innocently tried to introduce this into a conversation ... the slightest bit of sympathy for the people of Gaza and, well ... her uncle Alvin now refuses to speak to me.

RUTH
Tammy, can I speak to you for a second? Over here?

TAMMY
Because of that he thinks I'm antisemitic. I'm not. I've tried to tell him there's a world outside of the Middle East.

NED
(*to TAMMY*) You do like poking the bear, don't you?

TAMMY
That's my clan.

Angrily, RUTH moves off to the side.

RUTH
Tammy. Now!

Puzzled, TAMMY joins her.

TAMMY
What?!

RUTH
We are not going to get into this again. I've asked you to stop bringing this up.

TAMMY
I will not allow anybody, not even you, to silence my voice.

RUTH
You're a type 2 diabetic and you still drink Coke, and every time I criticize you for that, you tell me to shut up.

TAMMY
That's different.

RUTH
It's always different. Look, I may not fully or wholeheartedly agree with my uncle, but I respect him. He comes from Israel and so do his opinions. He also helped finance my first Starbucks. In a way, he's responsible for any house we may buy together.

From the other side of the room, the other characters watch TAMMY and RUTH.

NED
I remember arguing with my wife about inconsequential stuff ... like me leaving the toilet seat up.

ADRIAN
I don't think that's an issue in their house.

RUTH
And if we're gonna play that game, I've got some choice observations about your aunt Melanie. The opinions she's expressed about our relationship ... the things she's said to mc ...

TAMMY

All right. I get your point. But you know a lot of Jews are critical of Israeli politics, especially since the Israel-Hamas war.

RUTH

Then let them. In our universe, there's just me and you. And soon, Adam.

TAMMY

I told you I don't like the name ...

RUTH

I was hoping to discuss this at a later, more convenient time and place, but fuck it ... ever since you ... we ... became pregnant ...

TAMMY

What?

RUTH

Things are changing. I don't know why, but I have, too. Life's become more complicated.

NED

That's true. Kids will really fuck up your philosophies of life. God love 'em.

RUTH

It's been bothering me for a while now. He will be growing up into a world where there are people who won't like him simply because of who he is.

TAMMY

(*pointing at herself*) Hello! Mohawk!

RUTH

He needs to know history before he can move into the future.

TAMMY

Hello again! Mohawk!

RUTH
From what my mother told me, my father wasn't a very devout Jew. But when my sister and me came along, he began to attend services again. (*indicating NED*) As he so eloquently said, children can make you start wondering less about yourself and more about the world. I would like our child to know his Jewish half. And in order for that to happen, I have to know it myself.

TAMMY
Is that why you want to learn my language?

RUTH
I was hoping it would ignite a passion in you.

TAMMY
I don't need any passion ignited in me. I'm Kanien'kehá:ka 24-7.

RUTH
I meant a passion for what I can give our child. If I spoke your language, maybe you'd ... just a suggestion ... join me in keeping ... kosher.

NED
Does anybody have any popcorn? This is getting ...

EVE
Shh.

TAMMY
And give up corn soup and meat pies?! That's cruel.

RUTH
The guy ... guy-younga ... younga ...

TAMMY
(*angrily*) Just say Mohawk.

RUTH
You ... they never had pork. So you can't claim that's some form of traditional cuisine. If you say no, I can't help thinking you believe your traditions are more important than mine.

TAMMY
Of course I don't ... it's a fucking bowl of soup! And why do you keep referring to our child as a boy. We don't know anything yet. Are you pulling some sort of patriarchal shit on me?

RUTH
Well, everything you've told me about Indigenous women and what has been happening to them in this country, and everything I see on the news, the tragedy, the horror, it makes me worried. If it was a daughter. (*pause*) It might be better ...

TAMMY
Don't finish that sentence. (*taking a deep breath*) Later. We'll talk about it ... later. Like you said.

ADRIAN's phone rings. They all look to him. Reluctantly he turns his phone off.

ADRIAN
Not right now. It's too much. In the words of a famous antebellum princess, "After all, tomorrow is another day."

EVE
I seriously thought this day would end a lot differently.
I really did.

NED
I'm not sure, but I think he's hit puberty. His balls just dropped.

ADRIAN
I may have just ruined my life. But at least I'll have a nice place to live.

NED

Yeah ... the power of positive thinking and all that. But I wouldn't take out that bank loan just yet. Ms. Rhodes will have some offer juggling to do.

NED gives EVE a conspiratorial thumbs up motion.

ADRIAN

(*to himself*) I'm fucked.

NED

Well, with you being "fucked" aside, I'm curious. I've talked about my limited but existing connection with China, and no way you can miss this lady (*indicating TAMMY*) feels her connection to the land and this house is way more important than ...

TAMMY

(*interrupting*) I never put it like that!

NED

... ours, but you. I've had a few drinks with some fellows of the Black or African diaspora. And if I remember correctly, they do not carry much nostalgia for what euphemistically was called the Dark Continent.

ADRIAN

Oh come on, of course not. Most Black people don't know what part or parts of Africa their ancestors came from. There is no personal connection with Africa, any more than she (*indicating TAMMY*) would have with Siberia.

EVE

Siberia? I thought you were Indigenous?

ADRIAN

Yeah, there's this migration theory I read about in university.

TAMMY
Oh that. You're being awfully forgiving when you use the term "theory." But since you opened Pandora's box, due to conflicting archeological evidence, some actually believe Indigenous people migrated across the Bering Strait, Siberia to Alaska, some ten to fifteen thousand years ago.

NED
Welcome to the club.

TAMMY
Thanks, but no thanks. We believe ... and I think I can safely say this about all First Nations people, that we've been here a lot longer than that. We call the Bering Strait theory the BS theory.

RUTH
Get it?

NED
Yes, she's so subtle.

ADRIAN
Maybe I should phone her back.

NED
Oh for Christ's sake ... (*looking at RUTH*) ... oh, sorry.

RUTH
No problem. I know He's built up quite the fan club.

ADRIAN
I mean, Jen's not well. I sort of forced this move. The Caribbean community is quite strong out here. My father was from Trinidad, but he never really talked about it much. Jen always was ...

NED
Stay strong, my friend. It's been said moving and buying a house are two of the most stressful events in a person's life.

Unfortunately, the two are usually entwined. Read that in a fortune cookie once. Ms. Rhodes, you've been unusually silent during these discussions. No comment?

EVE
I don't think it's my place to comment. Have some more cheese. Crackers, I think I have some more crackers ...

ADRIAN halfheartedly snorts.

EVE
What?

ADRIAN
You. Cracker. Never mind, you'd have to be Black to get it.

NED
Ms. Rhodes, you have no opinion on Palestine, Maafa, or the migratory patterns of Indigenous people?

EVE
I did earlier ... but I'm tired now. Besides, I'm just here to sell this house.

NED
In a crime-ridden neighbourhood?

EVE
It's not crime-ridden. My husband and I have lived here for over eighteen years and ...

Silence.

RUTH
Aha. Eighteen years. So you're not a real estate agent? You actually live here.

EVE
(*pause*) It's complicated.

TAMMY
I don't understand.

ADRIAN
I don't either.

NED
I thought you knew a little too much about this house and the neighbourhood. Little things she's been saying ... what real estate agent knows the ranking of party candidates in the last federal election? Or the exact ethnic breakdown of the street? That's a little above and beyond the call of duty. Ms. Rhodes?

EVE
Okay. I am a real estate agent. Or I was. I gave it up. Retired. My husband gave up his job, too. We are looking towards new adventures, new challenges.

RUTH
And what did your husband do? For a living, I mean.

EVE
A real estate lawyer.

ADRIAN
So why all this ... subterfuge?

EVE
Well, we're entering a time in our lives where it's now or never. I'm more used to being the third party in these situations. I really didn't want to end up sharing our lives with everybody who walked through that door ... unlike you people. You know, people asking, "why are you moving?"

NED
Why are you moving?

EVE

Well, I don't really think that's relevant to the issue right now, do you?

NED

But I'm curious. I think we're all curious. We've all been dragged into this ... I don't even know what you call this.

TAMMY

First things first. Is this house actually for sale?

EVE

Yes, it is. Very much. We're going to use the money for the next stage in our lives. As much as possible. That's why I'm selling the place myself. I had some leftover real estate signs in the garage and, well ...

NED

Oh, I so want to hear this. New lives?

EVE

Fine. We're moving to New York, where I plan to be an actress and my husband will be a playwright.

TAMMY

An actress and a playwright. In New York City. Broadway and all that?

RUTH

How old are you guys?

EVE

You are not the first to point out how difficult this may be. But we've made our decision. Selling this house will give us the opportunity to get settled and ... get our new careers started. We have high hopes for our future. I've been taking acting classes for three years and ...

Silence.

What? We're not allowed to have dreams?

TAMMY
Holy, your glasses are so rose-tinted, it's amazing you can see out of them.

EVE
I beg your pardon?

TAMMY
I think we can safely say we ... as a group?

Everybody nods.

TAMMY
... have completely different priorities in our lives.

EVE
This is because I'm white, right? For the record I'm not white, I'm Celtic! And our heritage is completely irrelevant to the selling of our house. My husband and I have spent most of our lives playing by the rules. Our children are gone, both of us are bored with our jobs and lives. This is our time now. We've earned it.

RUTH
Break a leg, Ms. Rhodes. Can we leave yet?

NED
(*looking out the window*) Cops are still there.

ADRIAN is looking at his phone.

ADRIAN
Hmm, only thing I can find online says, "The police have blocked off streets in a two-block radius of this address due to an unknown criminal activity. People are urged to stay inside until further indicated." That's wonderfully vague.

EVE is looking very overcome.

EVE
Oh my!

ADRIAN
Ms. Rhodes, is the family that lives there ... what colour or nationality are they? Black? White?

EVE
Really, I'd rather not ...

ADRIAN
Ms. Rhodes, please don't take anything personal from this. Some of our best friends are white. In fact we have a white person that comes and cleans our house twice a month. She's hardworking and punctual. I'm not sure if she's Celtic, but ...

RUTH
Actually, us too. Michelle. I think her last name is French.

EVE
Enough. I've tried to hold my tongue in the midst of all this, but seriously, all this white bashing can be quite rude and traumatizing. I'm not sure I want any of you living in this house.

NED
The house that's going to pay for your career on Broadway?

EVE
Shut up. You don't know me. You have no idea what I or my husband are capable of. This house didn't buy itself. We worked hard to afford this. Nobody is handing us our dream. We plan to work for it like we did this house.

NED
Ah, the American dream. You'll fit right in.

EVE

Keep all your criticisms of white people to yourselves. What they did is what they did. What I am doing is what I am doing. I can't put it any simpler than that. And ... and ... and you probably don't want to believe it, but even people like myself, yes me, have sampled marginalized cultures. Back in the 2000s, we toured a kibbutz. In India we stayed in an ashram. We didn't like it, but that's not the point. We make a habit of supporting cultural tourism. As much as possible. But still, I am not responsible for anything you are talking about. Neither me nor my family had anything to do with Gaza. Or the Chinese head tax. Or residential schools. Or slavery. Or anything else that seems to be wrapped around our collective neck. I just sell houses, or used to, and now I want to be an actress. (*looking at her watch*) And it looks like I'm going to miss half hour. Sam's going to kill me.

NED picks up an empty bottle of wine, looking disappointed.

NED

I would salute you, but ... I never had dreams. I was told they just got in the way.

RUTH

I wouldn't tell your son something like that.

NED

But dreams aside ... really, the Holocaust and slavery? Colonization? You bring those up. Haven't those cards been played to death?

ADRIAN

I don't think that's possible. Those are ... those are ... they're pretty big cards.

NED

Has anything new or innovative been said or written about them recently? You guys need to forget that shit and move forward.

ADRIAN

"You guys?" Your descriptive eloquence is overwhelming, but I'm having trouble seeing ...

NED

You can stop right there. Don't forget, I'm a "you guy," too ... (*pointing to his eyes*) Not specifically your kind of guy, but still, to Canada, I'm one of "you guys." And my people came here with the specific purpose of moving forward. Seeking their fortune in this new land, as ludicrous as that may sound. We built your fucking railroad. Supposedly there's a dead Chinese man for every fucking mile of that railroad ...

TAMMY

Built on our land.

NED

Your land? I didn't realize Mohawk or Kaha ... Whatever, extended to BC and the prairies.

TAMMY

Stolen land is stolen land.

NED

And here you are, talking about stolen land but buying half an acre of that land back. Is that more of the irony you love?

ADRIAN

I saw this documentary once show how an awful lot of Black people used to run those trains you speak of. Porters and all. But like you say, that was then and this is now. Today I don't think people cross the street when they encounter an Asian man walking down it. Or move away when you move in.

NED

Okay. Fair enough, but we have our own issues. Do you know the worst part of being Chinese?! They expect you to open a Chinese Canadian restaurant in every fucking small town across this country. You know, there's one on Fogo Island ...

RUTH

Off Newfoundland, right?

NED

A tiny island in the middle of the Atlantic. Farthest east you can go in this country. And the farthest west, Haida Gwaii, the small town of Masset, population something just over 2,000 or something when I was there twenty years ago, has, like, four Chinese food restaurants.

EVE

Why so many if it's such a small town?

NED

I think Native people love Chinese food.

RUTH

It's true. They do.

TAMMY nods.

NED

All to make Chinese food that isn't even real Chinese food. Sweet and sour chicken balls! I mean ... what the fuck is that glowing orange sauce made of?! Chop suey ... most Chinese coming over from China have never heard of it. And if you want your computer fixed, the going belief is "call a twelve-year-old Chinese boy." What pisses me off about that is ... it's true! Whenever my computer fucks up, I have to call my son, and believe it or not, he's Chinese.

NED pauses for a moment, almost looking vulnerable.

And full disclosure, I've never been to China. Japan, yeah. India, yeah. But not China. Never had a need or desire. I'm not sure what that says.

TAMMY
There are worse things than people believing you can defend yourself and are good at computers. My people are supposed to be unemployable, poverty-stricken alcoholics. So you'll have to excuse me for not shedding a tear about that.

RUTH
(*holding her hand up*) Money-hungry, cheap, secretive, running the world. Great doctors and lawyers. Bad athletes.

ADRIAN
Undereducated, lazy, fatherless, gangbangers ...

EVE
Don't forget big dicks.

They all look at EVE.

EVE
We're talking about stereotypes, aren't we?

ADRIAN
Sort of, but that's a long story. (*pause*) Maybe a true one but ... okay, what if your community doesn't think you're Black enough ...

NED
Oh really?

ADRIAN
What? You can't measure things like that. Anyway, I am the lead chef in one of the top-rated restaurants in the city, not playing football or basketball – you're called an Oreo. Black on the outside, white on the inside.

TAMMY
Apple.

NED
Banana.

EVE
I'm lost.

RUTH
I wish it was that simple. It can get complicated for the secular Jew. There's non-denominational, trans-denominational, post-denominational, or just plain Jewish. Then there's orthodox, conservative, reformed, Ashkenazi, Sephardic, and so on. There's a cornucopia of options.

EVE
Okay, I have a stupid question.

Everyone looks at EVE.

RUTH
Yeah?

EVE
I'm a little confused. When you walked in, I thought you were white. I admit it seems a moot point right now. But Jews ... didn't Christians come from the Jews? And there are all sorts of Jews in Eastern Europe. And in Ethiopia. I've seen them on TV. Those ones look Black. (*to ADRIAN*) No offence.

ADRIAN
Of course not.

EVE
Are Jews considered a separate race or just a separate religion? I've always wondered that.

RUTH

You are not alone. The nazis thought we were a separate race. Some in this world think we're white. Others not so much. The right wing seems to think we're a legitimate and separate race, while the left wing thinks we're just a religion claiming to be a unique people. Depends who you talk to.

EVE

Well, which are you?

RUTH

You tell me.

There is an ominous silence. Outside the window, the lights from one of the police cars begins to move and gradually disappears. They all notice.

RUTH

This could be something good.

EVE grabs her handbag and puts her husband's script in it.

NED

Thank God. I want out of this zoo.

TAMMY

Now, about the house, we'd ...

EVE

No.

Everybody pauses.

TAMMY

I'm sorry. I don't ...

EVE

No. For the last hour, I have been listening to you all go on and on, and I have remained quiet. But ... but ... but ... I have to ask, what about the segment of Canadian society who are like me?

NED
Sorry. What?

EVE
You keep talking about oppression and how society has treated your people. What about me? My people. I mean, we haven't had it easy. Maybe a lot worse than what you're talking about. And a lot longer.

RUTH
Realtors?

EVE
No. Women. We could be here all night if I were to list the litany of wrongs perpetrated against women ever since recorded time. And even to this day. By men. (*to TAMMY and RUTH*) Am I right, sisters?

RUTH
Oh please don't.

TAMMY
No, no, no, no. While I support what you are saying in general, do not include us in your path of validation. My journey as an Indigenous woman is so far removed from yours as a white one, oh God ... where to begin? I don't know many Indigenous women who would pack up their lives and move to another country to start a whole new career that is notoriously hard to begin with, in the hardest place on this planet to start. At the age of what ... sixty?

EVE
Fifty ... two.

TAMMY

Sorry. I've never been very good at judging Caucasian women's ages. But you don't have optimism, you have delusions.

EVE

Ms. Maracle-Brummer, do you really think we, as women, have no connection?

TAMMY

There's a connection, it's just tenuous.

EVE

There's nothing tenuous about vaginas and breasts. We talk, you know. I can't believe Indigenous and Jewish women aren't interested in the same things I am and all the other women I know.

TAMMY

Like what?

EVE

I am a business woman and an actress. Do you know how few of us are out there making a difference? All that glass ceiling, gender parity, sexual harassment, pay equality stuff. Those are issues that affect all of us. Both of you included.

RUTH

Normally, I revel in the power of the Y chromosome. But it's easy to be kind and forgiving looking down the social ladder. Harder looking up.

TAMMY

Everything you just mentioned is important. But that is more of a white women's feminism wish list. Those of us in the minority trenches have a different set of priorities. Issues involving Missing and Murdered Women and Girls. Cultural survival. The fact that many of our men don't address their responsibilities involving children. Being a Native woman is a complex thing.

RUTH

And Jewish. It's a matriarchal culture, but the more orthodox your community is, the less power you're allowed as a woman.

EVE

And being a white woman ... I can't believe I'm saying that ... can't be complicated?

TAMMY

Rez and suburbia politics. It's like swimming and riding a bike. Both equally complex, just using different muscles.

EVE

I have climbed as many mountains as you have. Fought as many battles as you. I refuse to believe I have anything to be ashamed of.

TAMMY

I assume those were first-world mountains and battles.

EVE

I don't think I want you to live in this house. Please leave.

RUTH

The police are ...

TAMMY

I don't give a fuck. This won't be the first police blockade I've crossed. Let them shoot me.

RUTH opens the door and police lights flood in. TAMMY looks to RUTH.

TAMMY

Are you going to grab your jacket?

RUTH weighs the situation, then grabs her coat.

TAMMY

It's a good thing I love you. We'll find a home somewhere else. Let's go.

RUTH

(*to EVE*) You have a very nice house. I hope to live here. She'll calm down and I will talk with you on Monday, once the dust settles. I think you'll find we can be quite financially competitive. (*smiling and winking*) You know what they say about us Jews.

RUTH walks past TAMMY. Annoyed, TAMMY follows, closing the door. ADRIAN, NED, and EVE go to the window.

EVE

She was very rude. I'm surprised that woman can live with her.

NED

You get used to it. And then you stop getting used to it. I know.

EVE

They've made the sidewalk.

ADRIAN

What do you mean, "You stop getting used to it?"

NED

Growing up, my parents told me I had to be better than those around me. But at the same time, don't draw attention to myself. Be a good and observant boy. So every day after regular school, I went to Cantonese school. I can do Chinese calligraphy with a brush. Not a lot of call for that today. Haven't picked up a brush in decades. I married a good Chinese girl my family picked out for me, all unofficially, of course. She came from a very good family, I was told.

ADRIAN

I thought people couldn't or didn't do that anymore.

NED

What did you say … "Have you ever been Black?" Have you ever been Chinese?

ADRIAN

When I was seven. For Halloween. Went as Bruce Lee.

NED

You were probably better at kung fu than I ever was. How can I put this … my wife and I were aimed at each other by our families. It was always assumed we'd end up married. It wasn't an arranged marriage or anything like that, but in our culture, you try not to disappoint your parents. Whatever, my wife was very shy … in public. But at home, I'd return from work, and she'd have an actual list of her disappointments. My parents loved her. I, it seemed, wasn't living up to the individual my parents had sold her on. We were married for twelve years. Then I said, "Fuck it." I'm alone now. Both my parents are dead, and I'm divorced. I have no one to be observant or responsible to. Just myself and my son. My upbringing was more Chinese than Canadian. My father left China when he was a child. In a lot of ways, he never really left. He definitely wouldn't have wanted my son to play hockey, well, he's playing hockey. And I'm late for picking him up. Time for me to go. If it's okay, I might bring him over to see the place.

EVE

No. I don't want any of you living in this house. Please leave. Both of you.

NED

Really? Sure you're not just saying that, hoping we'll pay more to overcome your reluctance? Trying to gain your favour with a little extra money? You forget, you mentioned you've been selling houses for years. You know all the tricks. So do I. We'll talk.

EVE doesn't answer. In fact, she looks away. NED opens the door to the house and the room is filled with police lights again.

ADRIAN
You sure you want to go out there? Just because they ...

NED
Hey, I've done nothing wrong. And I'm not exactly running a gauntlet. I'm just walking to my car.

ADRIAN
I wish I had your confidence.

NED
Get angry. You will. Ms. Rhodes.

EVE
Mr. ... I'm sorry. Your name ...

NED takes out his business card and writes a number on it, handing it to EVE.

NED
Ned Leong. It's been a long day, Ms. Rhodes, and you've been stressed. Don't close all your doors. (*whispering*) Remember my offer. And I know some nice restaurants on 44th Street, just off Broadway.

As NED winks, EVE takes the card, looks at it, and reacts with surprise.

NED
And I am hoping this police situation is a rarity on this street.

EVE
Honestly, this is the first time this has happened in the eighteen years ... in the eighteen years we've lived here.

NED
Goodbye then, and wish me luck.

NED walks out the door, closing it behind him. EVE and ADRIAN watch through the window.

ADRIAN
So far so good.

EVE
I guess that means we can all go.

ADRIAN
So it seems. Eve, please don't include me with them. I'm sort of committed here, and I want to take this further. I totally understand where you're coming from when you talk about being a white woman. I used to date one. Actually, I've dated several. Okay, my wife is white. So I'm sympathetic.

EVE
I think that's only an issue if you make it an issue.

ADRIAN
Maybe, but it's been pointed out to me that it ... maybe ... is part of a larger issue. I've been on a journey, trying to find things out, about who I am and my culture. My parents weren't exactly enthusiastic about my interest. Anyway, things got a little heated here, and I'm sorry if I said anything offensive. And I want to make you a serious offer. Our Vancouver house should close in two or three days, and ...

EVE
Mr. Marshal, thank you for your interest. I'll discuss it with my husband.

ADRIAN
I won't give up, Eve. I want this house. I will have this house.

EVE

What about your wife?

ADRIAN's phone goes off. He looks at it for a second, then ignores it.

ADRIAN

That is a very good question. I don't know. (*putting on his jacket*) I always try and be positive. She's Swedish. She tells me they're a forgiving people.

EVE

The Vikings?

ADRIAN

I wanted to be an actor once. I think everybody does when they're young ... or older too. That way you can be whoever you want to be. Uh, the play you're in, I assume your husband wrote it, I don't know why I'm asking but, what's it about?

EVE

Oh just your usual postmodern exploration of the absurdities of contemporary life juxtaposed with societal expectations. That kind of thing. I think it's a comedy. He doesn't see it. I love him deeply, but sometimes the realities of life escape him.

ADRIAN

I envy that. (*looking outside*) I guess it's my turn. The police seem to be in a good mood. Wish me luck, a Black man crossing a phalanx of cops.

EVE

I'm sure you're exaggerating, Mr. Marshal.

ADRIAN

One final question, Ms. Rhodes. My wife is quite curious. The colour of the walls ...

EVE
White.

ADRIAN
Just white?

EVE
Just white. Simpler that way. White goes with everything.

ADRIAN
So I've been told. (*pause*) Goodbye, Ms. Rhodes.

ADRIAN leaves and closes the door behind him. EVE quickly gathers up the wine bottles and cheese remnants. She turns off the lights and takes a final look around before opening the door. Suddenly, a siren can be heard and EVE stops in her tracks.

EVE
Son of a bitch, the police did stop him. (*reacting as things escalate outside*) Hey, don't do that! He didn't do anything. He's been with me. Leave him alone!

She runs out, yelling.

Lights down.

The end

DREW HAYDEN TAYLOR is an award-winning playwright, novelist, filmmaker, and journalist. Born and living on the Curve Lake First Nation in Ontario, he has done everything from performing stand-up comedy at the Kennedy Center in Washington, DC, to being artistic director of Canada's premiere Indigenous theatre company, Native Earth Performing Arts. He is also known for his popular documentary series on APTN, *Going Native*. *Open House* is his thirty-sixth book.

PHOTO: PAUL CHATO